TALES AND
OF
WINDERMERE

by
Peter Nock

ORINOCO PRESS

Tales and Legends of Windermere

First published in 1989 by the
Orinoco Press
41 Oakthwaite Road
Windermere
Cumbria LA23 2BD

2nd edition completely revised and reset 1991

3rd edition 1999

4th edition 2002

Printed by
Middletons of Ambleside

Copyright © P.L. Nock 2002

ISBN 0 9514778 1 1

This book is sold subject to the condition that it shall not, by way of trade or otherwise, be lent, resold, hired out or otherwise circulated without the publisher's prior consent in any form of binding or cover other than that in which it is published and without a similar condition including this condition being imposed upon the subsequent purchaser.

CONTENTS

Crier of Claife 1

Calgarth Skulls 7

Robin the Devil 12

Drenched Souls 17

Horror at High Wray 21

Two Black Hands 26

White Cross Bay 35

Belle Isle 39

Conclusion 50

Bibliography 52

"The day-trippers... miss the real Windermere, fail to breathe with her wild woodland scents anything of the spirit of her winds and waters, see in the lights and shadows that shine upon and darken her silent reaches nothing of the tangled lights and shadows of her long history."

(E.M. Ward, 1929)

Front Cover Illustration by Christopher Cowell

THE CRIER OF CLAIFE

> *OF all the ghost stories associated with Lake Windermere, none is so darkly mysterious and so fraught with horror as the Legend of the Crier of Claife. Its origins lost in the mists of time, the tale has survived to the present day and is still widely believed locally.*
> *Claife Heights is the name given to the wooded fellside rising steeply from Windermere's western shore between the ferry and Wray. A pleasant enough place in summer, now well used due to its wide network of footpaths and bridleways, it can become lonely and terrifying after dark, when locals prefer to stay away.*

It was around the time of the Reformation. One stormy winter's night when the wind howled up the lake and the waves rolled northwards, a party of travellers were staying at the old ferry inn beneath Station Scar. They had postponed their crossing until the next day, and sat together in front of the roaring fire telling stories and jokes, the ferryman amongst them. Outside, the bare branches of the young sycamore trees moaned and whistled in the blast, while from time to time squalls of rain beat against the tiny windows of the inn. The ferry boat was securely tied to the landing stage opposite Crow Holme, the small island nearby.

The sound of a voice was suddenly wafted across the lake. The ferryman heard it first - he had an ear open for travellers through long practice. It was a prolonged wailing sound, only just audible above the wind, but plain enough to hear between the gusts. "Holloa! Boat! Holloa there! Boatman!" The long O's sang through the night across quarter of a mile of stormy water, at times merging with the wind, at times rising above it.

"Listen!" the ferryman cried. "Somebody's calling!" The chatter fell abruptly, and the room was filled with the sounds of the storm.

"I can't hear anything," someone declared.

"You've drunk too much ale, boatman," said another.

"No! Listen! I can hear it again!" the ferryman was persistent.

They fell silent again; and then, faintly, the sound of a voice was borne in.

"You can't go tonight!" someone exclaimed as the boatman drained his mug at one draught and rose to his feet.

"There's someone waiting, I'll have to go," he answered. "It may be a matter of life or death, if there's one abroad on a night like this."

He made his way to the door, some of the travellers accompanying him to the boat to see him on his way. Once outside, the blast of wind caught them suddenly. Through the interlaced twigs on the trees the scudding clouds were lit dimly by the intermittent glow of the moon over the far shore. "Expect me in half an hour!" he called, as he cast off and took the oars.

They watched as the boat set off across the waves; he had a fight on his hands to keep the heavy craft on course and stop it rolling in the troughs. The travellers went back inside the inn, full of admiration for a man whose devotion to duty could make him turn out for a passenger at so late an hour on so wild a night.

He steered by keeping the lights of the inn in line with the hill above. At other times a lantern was kept burning at the landing on Nab End, but tonight the storm had blown it out, and the dark trees which hung over the water's edge formed a particularly gloomy patch on the shore. And still that voice called out, unwearying: "Boat! Boat! Halloa there!" as if the traveller, whoever it was, could not discern the vessel creeping slowly over the water towards him.

"Alright, I'm coming, blast you!" the ferryman cursed as he pulled on the oars, his temper growing short. The voice had a mournful note about it which fitted in well with the dismal weather.

But at length, soaked through and chilled, he gained the lee of the Nab and came alongside the tiny stone jetty, looping a line through one of the iron rings set in the stonework. He stepped ashore, peering about in the gloom for his mysterious passenger.

"I'm here," he called. "Hallo! Are you there?" He walked a few steps up the road, his eyes searching the shadows in vain for some sign of his impatient fare, beginning to think the fellow had given up hope of a boat and gone away.

He shivered; it had gone unaccountably cold. A tall shape suddenly materialised out of the darkness before him. "Ah! There you are! Thought you'd given up, sir. Have you across in no time...."

But the words froze on his lips, the breath choked in his throat.

For a split second he stood stock still and gazed in horror at the abomination which leered at him in the moonlight.

Then, uttering scream upon scream he turned, rushed to the boat, loosed off, grabbed the oars and pushed panic-stricken into the lake. For what stood there at the water's edge, claws upraised to the sky, wailing and shrieking in devilish rage, was neither man nor beast but some loathsome creature from the very blackest depths of Hell.

An hour passed; two hours. The guests at the inn were becoming impatient, for the boatman was long overdue. And then, just as they were getting ready to go out and see what had happened and who the strange traveller might be, there came a sound at the door. The ferryman stood at the threshold. For a second, there was dead silence. Then a woman shrieked.

The fellow was scarcely recognisable as a human being: the expression of animal terror in a face which had aged twenty years; the hair that had turned completely white; the curious, whimpering sounds which he made, unable to utter human speech. They led him forward, offered him a drink, which he refused, tried to make sense of the delirious babbling which came from his lips, then put him to his bed and called a priest, who could do nothing.

For three days he lay in bed in a high fever, his face contorting with terror when anyone approached, shrieking aloud at times like a soul in mortal torment; and then he died without once becoming lucid enough to relate what had happened.

Of course they were not slow to guess the reason. The wretched boatman had encountered the Devil himself across the lake on that wild night. And thereafter, for night after night, whenever the storm winds blew, travellers putting up at the ferry inn would hear that mournful, wailing cry borne across by the wind: "Boat! Boat! Holloa there!" and they would shiver, cross themselves, bar the door, huddle more closely round the fire, take a drop more ale. No boatman would stir out after dark; punctually, well before sundown, the ferryboat was laid up for the night; nowhere on the entire lake would a boat put out while darkness held sway.

This state of affairs continued for many months, but eventually something had to be done. Legend has it that all the inhabitants went in a body to the priest on St Mary Holme with a request for help. If this were indeed the time of the Reformation, that priest would be one William Mountforth, a pious and venerable man who lived alone on the island; appointed by the King in 1510 to say mass for the souls of the long-dead de Lancasters, once lords of the Manor of Windermere. He did not refuse their request.

One stormy night when that mournful call was heard again from the Nab he set out alone in his small boat and rowed down the lake to that dread place. As his boat ran up the beach he took hold of his crucifix and boldly stepped ashore, repeating the name of the Lord. The fiend stood gibbering at him but was powerless to combat the spiritual power which opposed it. Repeating ancient prayers and exorcisms, the priest traced a circle round the Crier confining it within, and waited patiently for the dawn. That none might see the nameless being, he covered it from head to foot with his long cloak, and wound a rope tightly round. Then as dawn broke he took the monster in tow from his boat and rowed back to the chapel on St Mary Holme. There, in the presence of the entire population of Bowness - some say it was Christmas Day - he sang mass and performed the ceremony of exorcism.

This done, he took the fiend in tow yet again, this time heading for a spot on the western shore of the lake, deep in the woods of Claife. There, in a remote and lonely region far from all human habitation, lay a disused slate quarry. To this place, using ancient spells, he confined the fiend. The Crier was laid.

And yet, this was not quite the end of the story. Rumours began to spread around that on dark and stormy nights when the wind roared in the trees and the rain beat down on the fell, the Crier was permitted to leave his lonely den and roam through the woods, howling in concert with the gale, seeking whom he might once more terrify to death. And there were stories of men *"driven by despair or domestic discord"* who were seen wandering in that general direction and were never heard of again. One evening a local schoolmaster set off to walk over Claife from Colthouse to Belle Grange; he was never seen alive again. It was reported that packs of hounds, tearing in full cry through the dense woodland, would come to a sudden halt at the edge of the quarry and slink away whining; nothing would induce them to enter that apparently harmless place. The Crier will remain in his quarry, it was said, as long as ivy shall remain on the wall.

Not far from this quarry runs the old pack-horse road from Belle Grange to Hawkshead, traditionally known as the 'Bogey' Road. This connected with the Millerground ferry, and on the eastern shore of Windermere led up past Wynlass Beck to Applethwaite and thence on to Kendal. There is a story that one night some years ago a couple of poachers from High Wray were out in those woods, choosing perhaps to discount tales of the Crier. Suddenly for no accountable reason the air went icy cold, and both men were struck with a sensation of panic fear. Not staying to look round, they dropped whatever they were carrying and tore off through the trees faster than they had ever run in their lives, and have never returned there since, so deep was the impression made on them. It could be, perhaps, that some evil and malevolent creature does indeed roam through Crier Wood during the hours of darkness... certainly, local people from Hawkshead, Sawrey and Wray have some strange tales to tell of Claife.

One explanation of how the legend might have arisen was advanced in the 1860s by a local doctor turned antiquarian, Alexander Craig Gibson. He describes how he met an old woman of Cunsey who claimed to have actually heard the Crier. He expressed some doubt, but she had indeed heard the sound, as he was able to verify for himself. During a south gale the wind, as it rushes up the lake, is funnelled between the two opposing masses of Gummers How and Graythwaite Fell, so that when it reaches the ferry it comes in a strange, whistling noise, suggestive during squalls of a voice calling out above the storm. The sound is, apparently, *"...startlingly suggestive of the cry of a human being in extremity, wailing for succour."*

THE CALGARTH SKULLS

> *Calgarth Hall, not far from the modern Lakes Comprehensive School at Troutbeck Bridge, is one of the oldest buildings in Windermere, exceeded in years only by the parish church and the rectory. A tale of far greater antiquity than the Crier of Claife, the Calgarth Skulls is the story of how a wealthy land-owning family, the Philipsons of Calgarth, were punished by a dying curse and reduced to penury. The curse is still active even today.*

It was well after sundown when a fearful shriek echoed suddenly through the dark and lonely corridors of Calgarth Hall, the isolated manor house standing near the shores of Lake Windermere.

It was a shriek of pure terror, and the sound caused the master of the house, Myles Philipson, to leap to his feet and rush from the den where he had been counting his gold. He was met at the foot of the staircase by his serving man, white and shaking with fear.

"Well man, speak up! Was that you?" Philipson snapped at him.

In answer the fellow pointed dumbly towards the staircase down which he had so quickly fled. Philipson peered up into the gloom; there was nothing to be seen but shadows.

"Pah! Give me your light, fool! There's nothing there!" and taking the lamp from his servant, Philipson made his way up the creaking stairway.

But at the bend, where a niche had been cut into the thick, outer wall of the building, something which had not been there before caused the man to stop suddenly; and as he stared he turned pale, and felt the roots of his hair begin to prickle in his scalp. For there in the niche stood a pair of skulls, the sightless eye sockets seemingly turned towards him, grinning in grim mockery, the jaws agape in a sardonic leer.

Philipson knew well whose they were and why they were there. Some years ago, in 1565, his father Christopher had purchased the Calgarth estate outright and completed the Hall, thereby confirming his arrival amongst the ranks of the local gentry. He died soon afterwards, leaving Myles to extend the boundaries of his domain, which the younger man was all too keen to accomplish. There was one plot of land on the border of his estate towards Orrest Head which he was particularly anxious to acquire. This land belonged to an aged couple, Kraster and Dorothy Cook. In spite of repeated and generous offers they refused to sell until at last Philipson was driven to desperate measures to obtain the land on which he had set his heart.

He resorted to subterfuge. On the pretext of establishing friendly relations with his neighbours he invited the elderly couple to the Hall for dinner one day; and arranged that during their absence his servants hide a silver cup belonging to him in the Cooks' house. On their return he accused the pair of stealing his property which of course was 'discovered' in their possession. They were immediately arrested, arraigned before the magistrates, found guilty, and hanged as thieves.

In another version of the story the old couple were in the habit of visiting the kitchen at Calgarth Hall to cadge morsels from the owner's generous plate. On one such visit they were presented with a pie, inside which were concealed some silver spoons belonging to Philipson. As they returned home bearing the pie they were pursued by Philipson's servants, who had suddenly 'noticed' that these utensils had gone missing. The spoons were found and the astonished couple accused of the theft.

As the sentence of death was pronounced, old Dorothy Cook raised her hand and pointed at Myles Philipson. She and her husband would return, she shrieked; they would haunt Philipson and his family to the end of their days; the family's prosperity would decline, their fortune be lost, the house of Philipson would be reduced to ruin. When brought up to the scaffold, their last request before execution was that the chaplain read out aloud Psalm 109, in which the wrath of the Lord is implored against false accusers. Perhaps Philipson, hearing those words as he stood

Calgarth Skulls

waiting for the hangman to do his grim work, felt just a shiver of fear run down his spine.

He did not enjoy his ill-acquired land for long. As he gazed at the grisly sight on the staircase, Philipson knew the Cooks had returned to haunt him. Mastering his fear he at once gave orders for the skulls to be destroyed. They were taken away and buried. And the very next night there they were back again in that very same position. Enraged, Philipson ordered them smashed to pieces and reburied; but it was no good, they were back in place the next night, and for night after night the entire Hall resounded to a series of unearthly shrieks and groans, terrifying the servants and alarming the master.

Philipson, by now desperate, ordered the skulls to be flung into the deepest part of the lake, but to no avail; they were back again the following night in that same niche. The man was at his wits' end: the skulls were flung down a well; they were crushed into powder; burned in a fire; steeped in quicklime. Nothing would destroy them, they returned again and yet again, to stare out at him whenever he passed on the stairs, a mute and hideous reminder of the dreadful deed he had committed.

Legend does not relate what became of Myles Philipson. Thomas West, the famous guidebook writer, visited Calgarth in 1775 and reported that the skulls were still in place. James Clarke reported in 1789 that one of them had been removed to London. Since both were reliable writers it can safely be assumed that the skulls did in fact exist. Later writers have speculated on their provenance, from having belonged to a "Doctress" as a part of her anatomical studies, to being excavated from a supposed ancient burial site. By 1821 it was reported that only one skull remained, the other being almost entirely mouldered away - or presumably absent in London.

So perhaps that one remaining skull exists to this very day, walled up in its niche by the staircase, waiting for the curious investigator to break through the plaster and recoil in horror from the sightless grin, yellowed with age and frozen in the rictus of death. And perhaps the tales about their indestructibility really do have some substance. It is well-known in occult circles that a curse uttered by a dying person has an exceptionally powerful force; powerful enough, in this case, to contravene the laws governing the manifestation of physical matter.

The Cooks' cottage used to stand in the north-eastern corner of the junction of the Ambleside and Patterdale roads (A591 and A592), about half a mile from Calgarth, until it was demolished some time in the 19th century. This junction is known throughout the district as Cooks House corner, or simply "Cooks Corner", not to be confused with a culinary retail business of that name which trades in Bowness. It was said that in former times the Applethwaite gallows used to stand at this crossroads.

Calgarth Hall

That Myles Philipson was a genuine historical person is beyond doubt, for there are references to him in the Philipson family papers. Although the legend does not relate what happened to him after being haunted by the skulls, records tell us that the son of Christopher Philipson of Calgarth lived at Crook Hall, the family's senior residence, in the later 16th century. The family fortunes did indeed begin to decline, although not until after the Civil War, when vast sequestrations and fines were imposed on the gentry who had supported the Royalist cause. The Philipsons never recovered their former wealth and influence; by the late 17th century one of the family had fled to the American colonies to escape his creditors, another was in Appleby gaol and later in the Fleet prison in London.

The curse on the house of Philipson lingers to the present day. Calgarth Hall is now owned by the Hedleys, who rear Arabian stud horses, and the animals may often by glimpsed from the lake grazing the nearby fields. Mr Donald Philipson, a local descendant of the original family, related in a television programme some years ago how his eldest daughter, being fond of horses, worked for a while in the stables at Calgarth. She was unable, however, to continue in her employment. The horses became restive whenever she approached them: on one occasion she was kicked and severely injured, and on another she was trampled, although the animals remained perfectly docile when handled by her on other parts of the estate. No explanation has been advanced for this unusual behaviour, other than that it is associated with the ancient family curse.

ROBIN THE DEVIL

> *The story of Robert (Robin) Philipson's ride on horseback into Kendal Parish Church is well authenticated, and the siege of Long Holme reminds us that even comparatively remote places like Windermere could still be touched by the Civil War.*

Windermere's largest island, Belle Isle, was originally known as Long Holme. Some time during the 16th century this island, which had for many years been a waste, came into the possession of the Philipson family, and in 1566 Myles Philipson inherited it. Myles represented the Crook branch of the family, and indeed Long Holme remained with the Philipsons of Crook (rather than of Calgarth) throughout the troubled 17th century. In the period immediately before the Civil Wars Long Holme was the residence of Myles' two grandsons - Huddleston (who was born in 1621) and his younger brother Robert. The house where they lived seems to have been the near the site of the present round house, and may well have been fortified in some manner, since cannon balls were discovered there whilst the foundations for the present building were being excavated. These military associations, of course, refer to the time of the Civil War.

The Philipsons, being local gentry and land-owners, naturally supported the Royalist cause, as indeed did the entire county. The town of Kendal was the only exception, managing to maintain its adherence to Parliament while surrounded by a strongly Royalist countryside. Christopher Philipson of Calgarth served as a major in a regiment of foot, although declaring that he *"never marched out of his own country"*. The Civil War, however, touched Windermere (and Kendal) in a unique and memorable way.

Robin the Devil

The battle of Marston Moor in July 1644 resulted in the collapse of the Royalist cause in the north. Many of the defeated northern gentry managed to retreat to Carlisle, where under the leadership of Sir Thomas Glemham they regrouped to form a fresh nucleus of opposition to Parliament. They were presently joined there by members of the local Cumberland and Westmorland gentry, including the two Philipson brothers from Long Holme - Huddleston and Robert. However, by October the city was invested by a Scottish army (who were in alliance with Parliament) under the command of Lt.-General David Leslie.

Isaac Tullie, a young man who was present during the siege of Carlisle, left an interesting if rambling account of the occasion, referring to *"Captain Robert Philipson"* and *"Coronett"* (ie. Cornet) "Philipson", though he does not mention Huddleston by name. Both brothers seem to have been active during the siege, taking part in numerous sallies against the Scottish forces, and one of them on a secret mission to the King the following March, was captured at Wetherby, taken to York, and sentenced by the authorities to be racked for military information in his possession. Fortunately he escaped by climbing a wall, and presently made his way back to Carlisle. This sounds very much like an exploit of 'Robin the Devil', as Robert Philipson came to be known.

The siege continued throughout the spring and early summer of 1645, and by June the garrison were reduced to eating horseflesh. In the middle of that month Huddleston was sent to York under a flag of truce to discuss the possibility of surrender, and his return to Carlisle coincided with news of the decisive defeat of the Royalist army at Naseby on June 14th. Clearly further resistance was hopeless, and Glemham surrendered the city to Leslie on the 25th. The Royalist gentry were then free to leave, and most of them rode to rejoin the remnants of the Royalist forces, suffering yet further defeat at the battle of Rowton Heath, near Chester, the following September.

The above sets the scene for developments which had been taking place at Windermere. Before leaving for Carlisle the Philipsons had collected all the family treasure and secured it in their stronghold on Long Holme. Meanwhile, a certain Colonel Edward Briggs of Kendal, a leading Justice of the Peace and a fanatical Roundhead, heard that Robert Philipson and his treasure were on the island, and resolved to capture them both, in the name (of course) of Parliament. Briggs was himself distantly related to the family, through the marriage in 1540 of Christopher Philipson to Elizabeth Briggs of Helsfell.

Accordingly, Briggs set off with a small force, bringing with him some cannon, and commenced to lay siege to Long Holme. It is assumed that this is the time when the organ at St Martin's (Windermere parish church) was 'cut in pieces' by a Roundhead party. The siege lasted some eight or ten days (which later writers amplified into months), until Robert was relieved by his brother Huddleston. The latter, on receiving news of Robert's plight, had immediately marched from Carlisle - the siege having been ended - and Briggs was forced to withdraw. The episode can plausibly be dated to the middle of June 1645.

Why Colonel Briggs failed to take Long Holme is unexplained. His attacking force cannot have been very large, but neither again could that of the defenders. Robert, apparently forewarned of Briggs' advance, had taken the sensible precaution of commandeering all boats on the lake, so that his enemy was unable to cross over to the island. Like the English Channel, Windermere was a superb moat; and in addition Long Holme was well defended with cannon. How the siege might have gone if Huddleston had not hurried to his brother's aid is uncertain. Briggs did not possess the means to wear the defenders down by a long siege, acting as he was in mainly unfriendly countryside and operating far from the main theatres of war. It is uncertain how long it would have taken to obtain vessels from elsewhere and then transport them to Bowness. A battery set up on Cockshot Point would be the most advantageous place from which to bombard the house, but would in its turn be exposed to flanking fire from the island. A more secure position would be on Furness Fells on the western side of Windermere, but this would necessitate conveying his pieces right round the lake (the ferry presumably being unavailable) and hauling them on rough fell tracks over difficult terrain.

On Huddleston's timely arrival Briggs had to abandon his action and retreat to Kendal. The story, however, does not finish here. The initiative now passed to Robert, and not for one moment did he hesitate to take advantage of the changed situation. The very next day, we are told, Robert with a handful of followers rode over to Kendal intent on revenge. It was a Sunday; and knowing the devout nature of his opponent Philipson headed straight for the parish church, where he hoped to find the Colonel at divine service. Briggs, however, had been warned in advance, and prudently chose to absent himself.

Robert Philipson then proceeded to ride on horseback into Kendal parish church in an act whose effrontery and sacrilege have never been forgotten local annals:

"He passed the watch and rode into the church, up one aisle and down another to sacrifice, one of them met him, whom I shall not name, but was dehorsed in his return by the guards and his girths broke, but his partners relieved him by a desperate charge, and Robin in a trice clapped his saddle on horseback and vaulted on him without girth or stirrup, killed a sentinel and galloped away returning to the island by two o'clock."

This passage is by Thomas Machell, to whom we owe the earliest account of the story. Machell was rector of Kirkby Thore, a small village between Appleby and Penrith, during the late 17th century, and his principal hobby was that of the antiquary - or local historian, as he would be described nowadays. In pursuit of his interest he travelled throughout the county of Westmorland, making copious notes and rough sketches on all items of interest that he saw or heard. In 1693 Bowness and Windermere received two visits from him. To him posterity owes the earliest description of Bowness and its surroundings, including the lake, as they were three hundred years ago, as well as the earliest authentic account of the siege of Long Holme.

After his escapade Robert Philipson became generally known as 'Robin the Devil', with a vastly enhanced reputation. He did not survive for long, however. Unable to forsake the adventure of military life, he is next heard of in Ireland, and there he perished shortly afterwards at the Battle of Wexford. Meanwhile, Briggs was in the ascendant, and although he seems to have taken no further active interest in Long Holme, he certainly continued his campaign against local royalists, and on two occasions (1646 and

1649) Christopher Philipson was fined for secretly aiding the royalist cause. As Parliament's principal representative in Kendal, Briggs was certainly in a position to lord it over the entire county. His triumph, however, was short-lived, for after the Restoration he was at the mercy of his numerous enemies, and was forced to flee, finding refuge at a secret location in Furness Fells. Westmorland had become too hot for him.

Following the depredations of the Civil War, the Philipsons fell on hard times. Both the Calgarth and Crook branches of the family suffered, and in 1702, on the death of John Philipson of Calgarth, without male issue and practically bankrupt, the family ceased to exist as such; the remaining estates were broken up and eventually sold to Miles Sandys of Graythwaite in 1729. The Philipsons of Long Holme fared little better. In 1673 Christopher, Huddleston's son, pulled down the earlier building which had survived the siege, and built a new house. This became known as Holme House, and Machell completed a sketch of it on his visit to Bowness. Although Christopher was a more respected member of the gentry than his Calgarth relations he, too, failed to clear his estate of continued financial troubles, and after his death it passed to his daughter Frances.

DRENCHED SOULS:
THE WINDERMERE FERRY

> *The sinking of the Windermere ferry in 1635 is undoubtedly the greatest tragedy ever to have touched the lake, causing a shock which reverberated through the entire district and was scarcely obscured by the excitements of the Civil War which followed so closely upon it.*

There has been a ferry operating on Windermere since the very earliest times, the first recorded mention of one being in 1438. The traditional route was always over the narrowest part of the lake, between Ferry Nab and Swines Ness, as the Ferry House promontory was known in ancient times. This was the route connected with the Crier of Claife legend, and the ferry here was known as the Great Boat, as opposed to the smaller, or 'La'l Boat' which operated across the widest part of the lake, in the north basin between Millerground and Belle Grange.

The Windermere ferry, however, is remembered for one particular incident which took place on the afternoon of Monday, October 19th, 1635. On that day forty-eight people drowned, a tragedy which was traumatic enough to leave an impression in local tradition which survives even today. What happened may be conjectured easily enough, although there were no survivors to leave an account. The ferry was crowded both with people who were returning from Hawkshead market, and also with guests who had attended a wedding between William Sawrey and Thomasin Strickland the previous day. The bride's mother and brother were among the victims.

That weekend Westmorland had some of its heaviest rainfall of the year. According to Wharton, the Kendal chronologist:

"Eighteenth of October 1635, the river Kent came into the Vestry. And 19th Thomas Miller, boatman, and 47 men and women were drowned in Windermere water, with 9 or 10 horses, having been at a wedding."

The rain had been followed, as so often the case in the Lakes, by gales. All Monday the wind blew from the south or south-west, and by the afternoon it had reached a full gale. There had been little traffic for the Great Boat that day. The heavy, flat-bottomed vessel had been difficult enough to control in the huge waves which rolled up the lake, and the narrow crossing was taking anything up to twice the time, it being extremely difficult to keep the vessel on course. Around late afternoon the travellers who had been to Hawkshead market began to turn up at the shelter. Burdened down with their purchases, they were anxious to reach home before dark, for some were travelling as far as Crook, Staveley or even Kendal. Their number included quite a few wedding guests, no doubt somewhat the worse for wear. So they piled into the boat, upwards of forty of them squeezed tightly together, the horses tethered at the bow and stern, ready to brave the storm and the waves, for the ferryman and his assistants were experienced oarsmen, and indeed passengers themselves were often required to lend a hand with the oars.

Slowly the Great Boat, laden to capacity, pulled out past Crow Holme and away from the shelter of the point. At once the full fury of the waves struck where they were piled up by the narrowing of the lake, and she began to roll horribly. The men on the sweeps struggled to keep the vessel on course. Water began to splash over the bows, and the passengers on the starboard side were soaked suddenly by a huge wave which struck the hull with a terrific smack, causing the boat to roll awkwardly into the following trough. The wind shrieked madly at them, tearing at their hats and their hair, making the tears start from their eyes. As the next huge wave approached, tilting the vessel over to port, the sweeps on that side bit deeply into the water, while those on the starboard were lifted clear. This had the effect of forcing the bows further round until the whole vessel was broadside on to the wind.

With the boat momentarily out of control, the next wave struck with the force of a sledgehammer. Some of the women started to panic, waving their arms in the air; others called on them to sit down and be silent, while yet others called on the Lord for deliverance. The men struggled to bring the boat under control, to get the bows round and out of the troughs, but it was a losing battle. The huge, unwieldy, overloaded craft could only answer sluggishly to the sweeps and the rudder. The approach of yet another great wave threatened to engulf all the passengers on the starboard side, and as the boat began to tilt they fell bodily over to port, not heeding the cries of the others to remain where they were. To add to the confusion, the horses, neighing in alarm, started pulling at their tethers, kicking out, rearing and plunging, so that several passengers were struck by flying hooves. The sudden increase in weight on the port side and the slow roll of the vessel as the wave struck could produce only one result. The port gunwale touched the surface and went under.

Slowly, majestically, relentlessly, the Great Boat overturned, sliding down into the waves, dragging her shrieking load with her. The screams continued a little while longer as the drowning people threshed round frantically in the surging torrent, but *'no succour, no reliefe afforded'*, and gradually the cries were extinguished as the waves closed over their heads, until only a few pieces of wreckage were left floating. One horse, one single beast, succeeded in breaking free and swimming ashore, and stampeded for three or four miles, frantic with terror, before being taken. A few travellers who had arrived late at the ferry inn stood rooted to the spot in horror, too late to do anything to help. The waves rolled on up the lake, dispersing wreckage, and later bodies, around Long Holme and Cockshot.

Strangely enough, the Hawkshead parish register contains no mention of the tragedy. That for Windermere is unfortunately missing for the years 1629-36, perhaps destroyed (as was the church organ) during the Civil War. The only surviving record is in Grasmere parish register, which gives the complete passenger list. The bride's mother and brother who were reported drowned were *'Gervais Strickland's wife, of Staveley'* and *'Rolland Strickland'*. According to the Hawkshead register William Sawrey and Thomasin Strickland were married on October 18th. A still-born child was buried the following July, while Thomasin herself died a few days later, and William Sawrey remarried in 1638.

The year 1636 saw the publication in London of a curious poem, entitled *'The Fatall Nuptiall'*, commemorating the disaster. Only one copy survives, to be found in the Bodleian Library at Oxford. Its author was, almost certainly, Richard Braithwaite (1588-1673) of Burneside Hall near Kendal. He was popularly known as 'Dapper Dick', and became a deputy-lieutenant of

Westmorland and a J.P. The introduction to the poem contains a brief account of the ferry and its sinking:

'Lanch'd had these scarcely to the medth of the water, being scantly a mile broad, but the Boat, either through the pressure and weight which surcharg'd her, or some violent and impetuous windes and waves that surpriz'd her, with all her people, became drench'd in the depths. No succour, no reliefe afforded, for Gods definite Will had so decreed: So as, not one person of all the number was saved: Amongst which, the Bride's Mother, and her Brother in this liquid regiment, equally perished.'

Braithwaite's poem did not receive the fame its author might perhaps have expected. A couple of years later there appeared another poem on a similar theme, this time a shipwreck occurring off the coast of Anglesey. The poem was Lycidas, and its author, then an unemployed Cambridge graduate, went on to become one of the greatest poets in the English language. His name was John Milton.

Perhaps the mouldering remains of the Great Boat still lie somewhere on the lake bed between Nab End and Ferry House. According to tradition, the bodies recovered from the lake were buried beneath the yews in the churchyard at Bowness, in the 'eight and forty row', which was cut into by the chancel extension in 1871. Among them was that of George Wilson, a Kendal attorney, who was found *'...A just weeke after, and same houre o'th day, ...untouch't and undisfigur'd.'*

It is perhaps difficult for us in the late 20th century - although by no means unaccustomed to accidents involving public transport - to comprehend the magnitude of a disaster which happened so long ago. It is as if today one of the larger pleasure cruisers on Windermere were to sink at the height of the season with the loss of several hundred lives. In 1635 there were no official standards of safety, and man, more so than today, lived or died by his own wit or lack of it. The event must have been a lesson to boat-builders and boatmen alike; certainly thereafter the ferry boats were smaller and more manageable, if the vessel now preserved at the Windermere Steamboat Museum is to be taken as a typical example. A century and a half later, William Gilpin wrote that the accident *'made such an impression on the country, as a century cannot efface.'*

HORROR AT HIGH WRAY

> *Mass murderers are not a 20th century phenomenon. They have existed throughout recorded history and - unfortunately for us - will continue to be recorded.*
> *Tucked away in the woodlands of High Furness, as peaceful a corner of rural England as anyone could imagine, such a monster appeared.... and killed, and killed again, and yet again. The year was 1671*

In a stone-built farmhouse in the village of High Wray overlooking the north-western reaches of Windermere, a young woman paused in the middle of her housework and clutched at her stomach. The pain had returned; worse, far worse than ever before. Uttering a low groan, she sank to her knees as a cramp of unimaginable agony seared through her bowels. Alone in the house, there was no-one to come to her aid.

Jane Lancaster, just newly married, had been troubled recently with stomach cramps and diarrhoea - no doubt a fever picked up in the dank autumn air. But never, never had it been this bad. She knelt, trying vainly to stagger to her feet, weak and dizzy, her bare hands scrabbling at the stone floor. Another spasm, racking her body as if her insides were being chewed by a white-hot demon. Her body burst into a cold sweat, enough to soak her clothes... and then a bout of uncontrollable vomiting.

Another pang shook her, and then another, and another, unendurable bursts of pain bursting through her entrails, mixed blood and excrement fouling her under-garments. Between bouts of vomiting she was aware of someone moaning, not realising that it was her own voice. 'Lord, forgive my sins,' her lips tried to form the words as she writhed on her own kitchen floor in unimaginable agony. Then, in a final, shuddering convulsion, her head fell back and her eyes rolled up in their sockets.

Hours later, her husband Thomas returned from Hawkshead. The stench hit him as soon as he stepped over the threshold, bringing a grim smile to his twisted features. His plan had worked: the bitch was dead. There were some onions hanging in the pantry. He took out his knife, slit one in two, rubbed the two halves together and put them to his eyes. Then, tears streaming down his cheeks, he ran to his neighbour's cottage and banged on the door, calling for help in his feigned grief.

Their turn would come next.

High Wray Farm

Many months later a horseman was riding along the old, rutted lane from Sawrey to Hawkshead, where it crossed the moss at Pool Stang before entering the village. Preoccupied with his thoughts, the traveller almost fell from his steed as the mare shied without warning at something it had scented. "Whoa now! Steady on, girl! What's got into you?" he called, stroking the animal's neck in an attempt to calm it. He dismounted and, taking the reins, led the beast carefully forward.

It was late in the day, darkness was falling, with a rising wind and the threat of rain in the cold air. He had just crossed Windermere by ferry, the boatman regaling him with tales of the horrendous sinking - just thirty odd years ago - when over forty people lost their lives, and the story had put him into a dismal frame of mind. But what had frightened his steed?

He peered warily ahead, straining his eyes. A huge, solitary oak stood in the marsh, the wind moaning through its bare branches. Something swung and creaked and rattled in the breeze. A malodorous stench suddenly assailed his nostrils, a whiff of something so rotten, so redolent of the grave, that he recoiled in horror. But curiosity pressed him forward again.... and when the rider recognised what he was looking at, a shudder of revulsion brought an involuntary cry to his lips. 'Aaaahh! In God's mercy!'

It was a corpse which hung there, a gibbeted corpse, the skin black and putrescent, bleached bone showing white through the threadbare rags, gnawed strips of flesh hanging from the skull, the eye sockets long empty. And even as he stared, revolted, a gust shook the human cage and made the chains rattle and squeak.

The traveller passed by, remounted and made for the nearby town. And later that night, warmed by the friendly fire and a tankard of ale, his belly full with meat, he asked about the unwholesome sight back on the moss. His curiosity was soon satisfied, for High Furness had never known such a tale of horror before.

A year or two back a certain man named Thomas Lancaster from Threlkeld in Cumberland had turned up in the neighbourhood. He had married a local girl soon after, and her father subsequently conveyed all his real estate to his new son-in-law as security for a loan which Lancaster had promised him. But the newcomer had other ideas. He planned to keep the money himself, and his new properties, by murdering his wife and her family. Yet even that was not enough. To divert suspicion from himself he had to make it appear that their deaths were due to natural causes - perhaps a fever of some kind. And he had to make it appear that the entire family - neighbours as well - had suffered from this fever, with himself, by extreme good fortune, as the only survivor.

The method he chose was poison, and the poison was arsenic.

Arsenic trioxide, popularly known as white arsenic, is one of the most violent poisons known to man. It has been a favourite of poisoners throughout the ages because it is both tasteless and odourless, can be administered in varying doses and - most important - is untraceable. (Fortunately this is no longer the case, as modern forensic science can easily detect the presence of arsenic in the human body).

Arsenic is toxic to all living cells. It acts by damaging the circulation in the capillary blood vessels, causing traumatic leakage of plasma, and the first tissues to be affected are invariably the lining of the digestive tract - the stomach and the intestines. The victim suffers agonising cramps, vomiting, diarrhoea, dehydration, the symptoms varying in severity according to the amount of dosage. A skilled poisoner might begin by administering the toxin in minute doses, mixed undetectably in food and drink, just enough to mimic the symptoms of a gastric upset so that the victim remains totally unsuspecting. Then the poisoner can strike, administering such a massive dose that his victim is often dead - horribly - within hours.

And this is what Lancaster had done: first to his wife, leaving her to die alone in agony on the kitchen floor; then to her father, her three sisters, a young serving boy, her aunt, her cousins and - to make doubly sure that he would not be suspected - to several of their neighbours at High Wray.

Most died - but some survived, for people exposed to small amounts of the poison can sometimes build a resistance which enables them to survive otherwise fatal doses. Yet in spite of all his precautions the finger of suspicion was pointed at him.

Lancaster was arrested and brought before the local magistrate, Sir Daniel Fleming of Rydal Hall. Fleming, on examining the prisoner, was instantly convinced of the man's guilt - there was both motive and opportunity - and had no qualms at sending him off to the nearest gaol at [appropriately] Lancaster Castle, there to await trial at the next assizes. In a letter to a friend, written the very day of committal, Fleming commented that Lancaster *"hath committed the most horrid act that hath been heard of in this countrey....I have committed him prisoner unto Lancaster Castle, and shall take what more evidence I can meet with or discoverr against the next assizes that he may have there a fair triall, and, if he be found guilty, such a punishment as the law shall inflict on such like offenders."*

He was indeed found guilty; and the law reserved only one penalty for murderers: death. Thomas Lancaster was sentenced to *"bee carried backe to his owne house att Hye-wray where hee liv'd: and was there hang'd before his owne doore till hee was dead, for that very facte then was brought with a horse and carr into Coulthouse meadows and forthwith hunge up in iron Chaynes on a Gibbet which was sett for that very purpose on the south syde of Sawrey Casey [causeway] neare unto the Pooll stang: and there continued untill such tymes as hee rotted everye bone from other."* In this at least, Lancaster was fortunate: some malefactors could be gibbetted *alive*.

There is still a farmhouse at High Wray, now a charming B & B, with nothing to tell of the appalling murders which were once committed there. The site of the ancient gallows on Colthouse meadows may still be visited, although there is now nothing to see, and the ancient oak which stood there has long since decayed. The gallows tree survived until 1850. It was said that a splinter taken from the rotting stump and inserted into a dental cavity was an excellent cure for toothache. The marshy land immediately south of the Sawrey road (B5285) is still known as Gibbet Moss.

Just over a century later the young Wordsworth lodged with Ann Tyson at Colthouse when he was a pupil at Hawkshead Grammar School, and would have been familiar with the ancient oak and its grim associations.

TWO BLACK HANDS: JOHN BOLTON OF STORRS HALL

> *Storrs Hall is a palatial building set in spacious grounds on the eastern shore of Windermere a couple of miles south of Bowness. It has been a hotel for over a hundred years, although guests may not be aware of the ancient curse which lingers over the place. So widely was this curse believed in Bowness that when the extensive Storrs estate came up for sale in 1887, the hotel and its grounds were strictly excluded from the purchase.*

It seemed to 'Colonel' Bolton, as he glided back to Storrs with the light airs of evening after carrying off first prize in that afternoon's regatta in his aptly named yacht Victory that he was the happiest man on earth. A wealthy merchant and one of Liverpool's foremost citizens, widely respected in his vast circle of friends and acquaintances, blessed with an attractive wife and a palatial home on the shores of Windermere, he had everything a man could hope for. "No," he had told his boatman when the time came, after several celebratory 'bumpers' of wine in Bowness, to return to Storrs - "No, lad, you go home and enjoy your evening. I'll sail her back myself - it's lovely on the lake."

It was a calm, still, clear evening on Windermere, the breeze that had enabled him to beat all comers in the regatta now having died away to the merest whisper - no matter that he drifted gently, hardly moving in the still air; it was a pleasure simply to be alive. The sun was just about to set, causing the edges of a few high, solitary clouds to glow as if on fire. He had the lake to himself: deserted on this still summer's eve, not another vessel in sight, hardly even a dwelling to be seen breaking the densely wooded shores. So still, so silent, it seemed a haunted lake.

A light breeze started to ruffle the surface, causing catspaws of ripples to spread over the water; and for the first time that evening Colonel Bolton felt vaguely uneasy. The slackening sail filled suddenly, the yacht surged forward; something cold tingled at the back of his neck. He looked round, wonderingly. There was no reason for that sudden, chill gust of wind. But wait! What was that over there.... just where the ripples were spreading? He strained his eyes in the gathering dusk. Was there something in the water - a log, a piece of driftwood, or something? No, it was moving. It was coming towards him. Something quite small, quite unremarkable really, not much bigger in size than a human fist... a hand. There were two of them: two small, dark objects, moving swiftly across the surface towards him. He stared in amazement, unconscious of anything else. The two objects grew steadily closer and closer, and as they neared he saw, with a sudden frisson of horror, what they were.

Two hands. A pair of human hands; nothing else, no arms attached, just two hands, a left and a right, severed at the wrist. They were a few yards from the boat, and.... oh, dear God! What was this? They were rising from the lake dripping - not water but.... some darker liquid. Bolton turned ice cold in every limb, frozen with fear, hypnotised by the loathsome spectacle. He watched as the hands left the surface and made through the air towards him, moving purposely as if part of an invisible body. Nearer and nearer they came, to clutch at his throat, he could feel the cold, clammy touch as they started to close, vice-like, round his neck.

A hoarse shriek rang across the lake from the terrified man. "Oh God, no! No! Sweet Jesus, have pity!"

A moment in time passed; silence. Wonderingly, Bolton put a hand to his neck. Yes, his throat was still there, his shirt still in place. There was nothing else. The hands had disappeared. But at that dreadful moment, when he thought he had breathed his last, he knew. He knew the owner of those black hands with the pink palms - he had known her, forcibly, in the days of his youth. Sweet Rebecca - Becky - the black slave whom he had ravished long years ago on the island of St Vincent, who had grown to love him and, when the time came for them to part... No, no, he would not think of it. He had forced himself, willed himself over the years to forget that dreadful deed.

It was quite dark when Bolton reached his boathouse at Storrs, only enough light left to make out the dim outline of the little naval temple standing into the lake at the end of the promontory. A lamp had been lit for him in the boathouse, and his wife and servants were waiting anxiously for him as he finally drifted alongside.

"Dearest! Where on earth have you been? What has happened?" But Bolton brushed aside his wife's enquiries and, shouting for wine, stumbled along the dim-lit path towards his baronial residence. He could, after all, hardly tell Elizabeth the reason for his sudden discomfiture, confess to his wife that he had once been with a.... negress. She would have been horrified, thought him depraved. And perhaps he was. He knew he had a violent, ruthless streak; he'd striven to suppress this trait, but at times it would take him unawares, and when aroused he could commit acts of monstrous sadism.

Look at that time only a few years ago, he recalled as he lay stretched out in his favourite chair, the decanter of port at his side - back in Liverpool, that duel with Major Brooks. It had taken place in the gathering gloom of a December afternoon. The major's shot had missed, but Bolton's aim was deadly accurate. He could picture to himself even now the shattered face, the right eye gouged out by the bullet which had lodged in his opponent's brain. Bolton should have hanged for that, but they'd dropped the charges - you couldn't just condemn a leading citizen, the man who, with England daily expecting a French invasion, had raised the first battalion of the Liverpool Volunteers - 'Bolton's Invincibles' - just for winning a duel, especially in the face of a challenge which no gentleman of honour could possibly have refused. Damn him - Brooks was a blackguard, he deserved everything he got!

But that hadn't been the first time. There'd been Becky, out in the West Indies. Back in his youth, not yet twenty, he'd been an intelligent and an ambitious young man. His firm had sent him out to the Caribbean to look after their interests, and there he'd laid the foundations of his own fortune. His roving eye had quickly picked out the charms of the young African slave girl before she was even aware of him. Inflamed with rum one night and used to getting his own way, he'd fancied something different and had the girl brought to his quarters. Shy and frightened, at first she'd resisted his advances, but he was strong and used to getting his own way; and the encounter could have only one result. Accustomed to the trollops of the Liverpool alehouses, the dusky skin and exotic scent of the black girl had inflamed and excited him, and once his heart was set on something, there was no stopping him.

And amazingly, they had formed a relationship; Becky had grown to love the strong, self-willed teenager whom she looked upon as a white god. He, in turn, discovered a tenderness in himself which he had never suspected. And so throughout his stay in St Vincent their relationship had prospered, flourished.... until the time came for him to return to England. In vain she had pleaded with him to take her along; but no, it could never be. To bring a black woman home with him, to England, to move with her in the polite circles on which he had set his heart - it could not possibly be. Besides, the monotony was beginning to pall. It was time to start looking for an English wife, a lady to complement his position in society.

Becky had clung to him to the very end, followed him down to the harbour where the pinnace waited to convey him out to the great West Indies merchantman bound for Liverpool. She tugged at his wrist; with an oath he cast her off. Really, it was so embarrassing, in front of all these people - all these good citizens of St Vincent who were seeing him off. She'd disappeared then as he descended the steps at the harbour wall and boarded the light pinnace. Ah well, that was the end of her.

But then, as the little boat bobbed over the waves towards the harbour mouth, what should he see but a human form making across the water to intercept him? He rose from the stern in amazement. It was Becky, swimming strongly out to sea - yes, she'd always been a bit of an athlete. "Go back, Becky!" he called as she neared the pinnace. "Go back, I tell you! You can't come with me - not to England!"

"John.... Johnny! Take me with you, I beg you! I can't live without you!" The plea in her voice, her tears as she implored him, would have moved another man's heart; but Bolton was made of sterner stuff. "Get back, girl!" he told her. "Be off with you! You know you can't come - there's no place for you in England."

By now she had reached the pinnace and grabbed hold of the gunwale, trying to haul herself aboard by main force. To Bolton's immense discomfort, the other sailors were smiling broadly at the spectacle of the young gentleman trying to get rid of his negro mistress. "Dammit, let go!" he exclaimed angrily, but she would not, she just clung there, her weight slowing the boat and tending to spin it off course. "For God's sake, go back, Becky! I'll miss the tide - I'll miss my ship!"

But nothing he said would avail. He could hear calls from the merchantman, too, as sailors prepared to hoist the sails and weigh anchor. "Boat ahoy!" there came a call from the quarterdeck. "Hurry up there, Mr Bolton, sir! We MUST catch the tide!" There were only minutes to spare to come alongside and heave himself and his baggage aboard. Still that damned negress clung to the gunwale.

A sadistic rage boiled up within him. With an oath, he drew the cutlass which he always carried with him and brandished it in the air. "Let go, woman, before it's too late!" he cried. But as the girl whom he had once loved showed no signs of letting go, he made a couple of feints with the weapon, to no avail. "Damn you to hell, I'll teach you a lesson!" he cried. The heavy naval cutlass, razor-sharp, whistled down towards Becky's wrist, shearing through the metacarpal bones at one blow. A shriek of pain and terror rent the air. Then, before the others could stop him, another vicious cut with the weapon, and the second hand was severed.

Wailing in despair, the negro girl drifted astern of the small pinnace, the stumps of her wrists flailing ineffectually at the water. The boat's crew were dumbstruck in horror. "Give way, you men! What're you waiting for?" Bolton's voice interrupted the shocked silence. "She deserved it - she wasn't worth troubling over."

The boat's oars bit into the water and she came alongside the large ship, Bolton clambered on board, his baggage was heaved up after him. He was only just in time, seconds to spare - already he could hear the faint strains of *'Blow the man down, bullies'* from the foredeck as the crew sang the refrain to weigh anchor. The pinnace cast off and started at once in the direction of the disabled swimmer who was treading water and losing strength rapidly.

But an even worse horror awaited. As the boat hastened towards her, something could be seen cutting through the waves. Attracted by the scent of arterial blood and the commotion caused by a wounded creature, a large predator was circling in from beyond the reef. The triangular dorsal fin moved nearer and nearer as they watched in horror; preoccupied with her own agony, Becky had mercifully seen nothing. The shark bumped her from below; weak with shock and loss of blood, she scarcely felt it; but she was not too far gone, when the ugly snout of the fish broke the surface, its great jaws clamped round her slim waist, to let out one single, pain-galvanised shriek of sheer terror. And then it was over.

From on board the merchantman Bolton watched in growing horror. "Dear God!" he murmured; but then, recovering himself, he made his way below to take solace with a bottle of rum. Already the ship had set sail and was heading home over the blue Atlantic. With the business contracts he had negotiated, Bolton was on his way to becoming a wealthy man. With the single-minded purpose of ruthless ambition he resolved to forget all about the negro slave girl and her bloody end; and being a determined man he was successful in his resolve.

But now, on that calm evening on Windermere, his bloody past had caught up with him at last. Never, for all his resolve, could he forget the icy grip of those hands on his throat; and never, he now knew, would he be able to sail on Windermere again.

A few days later, walking in the grounds one evening beside the lake shore, strolling along the little stone causeway towards the naval memorial - a favourite vantage point to watch the regattas - he saw that ominous pair of hands rising again from the water, and was forced to beat a hasty retreat. Windermere, the lake he loved so much, was lost to him.

All his life Bolton had traded in human misery. He had shipped slaves from the African coast out to the Americas, traded them for rum, tobacco, sugar which he shipped in turn to Liverpool, and grown fabulously wealthy in the process. And it was not only rum and other goods which crossed the Atlantic to

Tales and Legends of Windermere

England: it began to be rumoured that slaves were brought over as well, human cargo brought up Morecambe Bay on the high tide at dead of night, landed secretly at Greenodd, taken the short distance overland to Newby Bridge, then hurriedly re-embarked to be transported up the lake to Storrs, led to the cellars by means of an underground passage leading off from near the naval temple, and there loaded with chains, to be presently taken up and trained in domestic service - as porters, waiters, cleaners - anything which demanded brawn not brain, any menial task which the whites disdained to perform.

Storrs Hall

Their training complete, they were then farmed out to his friends amongst the neighbouring gentry - the Rawlinsons of Graythwaite on the opposite side of the lake were one such family. They had a negro "servant" who won local fame as Black Jack of Graythwaite. A superb athlete, he could swim across the lake both ways, which was then regarded as an exceptional achievement. But not only this, we are then told that he excelled in the field of scholarship. Black Jack taught himself to read and write, studied mathematics, and became a proficient musician. But alas, he was cut off from intelligent society by his race, his origins and rural isolation - although by no means ill-treated by his employer.

Two Black Hands

When one of the maids at Old Graythwaite Hall bore a child whose skin was of an unusually dark hue, Mr Rawlinson - instead of having the putative father horse-whipped and driven from the estate - permitted the couple to marry and gave them a cottage hidden deep in Graythwaite woods where, no doubt, they lived out their lives in domestic bliss.

In spite of what has gone before, John Bolton enjoyed much respect locally, indeed was held in widespread affection. In Liverpool he took an active part in local politics, where his house became the local Tory headquarters, and at Storrs he entertained Canning, then the member for Liverpool and a future Tory prime minister, along with other distinguished company such as William Wordsworth and Sir Walter Scott.

Enterprising as he was in both commercial and political circles in Liverpool, Bolton took no less an active part in affairs at Windermere. He organised and took part in sailing regattas, winning race after race in his yacht *Victory* - indeed, so successful a sailor did he become that many yachtsmen refused to compete against him. In 1836 he donated a new building for Windermere Grammar School (which had been founded some two hundred years previously), asking his friend Wordsworth to officiate at the opening ceremony; ever afterwards the arms of the school were those of the Bolton family.

Yet this philanthropic gentleman had acquired his wealth by trading in human misery. That he was involved in the African slave trade is beyond doubt: records show that in 1799, for instance, he owned two ships, the *King George* and the *John,* which plied the mid-Atlantic between Angola and the Caribbean. It is as well to remember that an interest in the slave trade was considered a perfectly normal and reasonable form of commercial activity, exciting little adverse comment. Black people were widely regarded as second-class human beings and were thought, like animals, to be incapable of feeling the same pangs of ill-treatment and deprivation as the more sensitive whites. Certainly in the Liverpool trading establishment where Bolton operated, his activities were regarded as perfectly normal and respectable.

It was only in more liberal circles that the anti-slavery movement was making its voice heard. It is perhaps ironic that its chief proponent, William Wilberforce, used to spend his holidays in the 1780s at Rayrigg, just north of Bowness. Rayrigg Hall then belonged to the Flemings of Rydal, to whom Wilberforce was related, and it became his favourite practice to row out to the nearby island of Lady Holme on summer mornings, to spend a few hours in quiet meditation amongst the remains of the old ruined chantry.

Quite apart from the two black hands which haunted Bolton, the real curse on Storrs allegedly dates from the time of his predecessor, Sir John Legard, a man who according to all reports was also deeply involved in the slave trade. The story goes that excise men effected a surprise raid on Storrs, and in the panic to get the black 'servants' out of sight and down into the cellars, one of them - a young boy named Tom - cried out. In the attempt to stop his mouth and prevent him giving the game away, his cries were smothered and he suffocated.

The boy's mother, mad with grief, levelled a curse on the Hall and all its future owners, to the effect that never should the property pass from father to son. And it never has. As with Calgarth, this is a curse which survives to the present day.

The boy was buried at St Martin's in Bowness, where his tombstone reads simply: *'Tom. A slave boy from Storrs Hall'*.

WHITE CROSS BAY

> *The visitor enjoying a cruise from Bowness to Ambleside will hardly fail to notice, at about the halfway point, a small white cross standing a few feet into the lake near the entrance to a small bay. The bay is White Cross Bay, and there is a tragic tale behind that solitary stone cross.*

September 13th, 1853, was a clear, sunny day on Windermere; the air was warm, the water calm, the lake sparkling in the mellow light of late summer. Two young men, visitors from Lancashire, were staying with friends in one of the Ambleside guest houses. The fine weather tempted them, instead of a walk on the fells, to venture onto the lake; the water looked so inviting, so peaceful.

The elder of the two was Ralph Thicknesse, a promising young man aged twenty, whose father was the M.P. for Wigan. His companion, Thomas Woodcock, 19, was a lieutenant in the 3rd Royal Lancashire Militia: on duty splendid in his scarlet uniform, but now casually attired in holiday wear. For their excursion the friends had chosen a light rowing skiff - such vessels could easily be hired on Windermere right up to the last war, although nowadays they are no longer available.

Ralph and Thomas set off to row to Bowness - not a vast distance, just under five miles in a straight line - and two young men rowing vigorously in a light skiff would cover the distance in well under an hour.

No-one can tell us what happened. Perhaps they had stood up to change places, always a risky procedure in a narrow boat; perhaps a breeze had sprung up and raised a few waves on an exposed part of the lake; perhaps their craft was leaky and they couldn't bail fast enough. But at some point as they were passing near a small bay known as Craams the boat went over, sending the two non-swimmers to the bottom. Two fine young men, promising careers before them, were no more; their holiday was at an end.

A small stone cross was erected to the memory of the two friends by their grieving relations. The base bears an inscription recording their names, the date of the tragedy, and a brief religious text: *Watch therefore, for ye know neither the day nor the hour.* [Matthew, 25, 13]

Unusually, apart from a mention in the Westmorland Gazette, the incident attracted little further attention, although Harriet Martineau, whose *Guide to Windermere* was published the following year, was almost certainly referring to it when she wrote:

'And nothing should induce him [ie. the visitor] to go out in one of the little skiffs which are too easily attainable here, and too tempting, from the ease of rowing them. The surface may become rough at any minute, and those skiffs are unsafe in all states of the water but the calmest. The long list of deaths occasioned in this way, - deaths both of residents and strangers, - should have put an end to the use of these light skiffs, long ago.'

As time passed the name of Craams Bay was forgotten. The place is now widely known as White Cross Bay - a caravan park, a popular lakeside holiday centre, and during the last war the site of a huge flying boat factory where the famous Short Sunderland aircraft were built and launched onto the lake.

The cross you can see today is not, however, the original one; this was lost some years ago, said to have been broken up and buried beneath tons of earth when the caravan site was extended. The latest version is only a few years old, but a fair copy of the original.

Some years ago an amusing spoof, reproduced opposite, was carried in a local paper. So realistic was the appearance of this document that it not only took in the paper's editorial staff but even a number of local historians. The perpetrator had apparently discovered a few sheets of extremely ancient, headed notepaper when the boat proprietors' old cushion huts at Bowness Bay were being demolished.

Private Address:
PEARL COTTAGE,
WINDERMERE.

BOWNESS on Windermere, 13 September 1854

Messrs Lloyds of London
Marine Underwriters

Copy J.C.

DR TO **JOHN CAMPBELL,**
Yacht & Boat Proprietor.

		£	s.	d.
To losses incurred during recent tempest on this water vicinity Kraams Bay resulting in nil fatalities, inter alia wiz:-				
Item:	1 Rowing Boat	10	10	0
	2 Rods on hire		2	9
	1 Can of worms			3
	1 Anchor		3	0
Item.	Provisions:			
	3 lb salted pork		1	0
	4 lb Bread			8
	2 lb Potted Char			9
	12 Botts. Madeira		14	6
	£	11	12	11
Less flotsam Salvaged.	1 Baling Can			3
	2 Gents. Velour hats		3	0
	£	11	9	8

COPY

One interesting feature of this part of the lake are the engraved rocks near Ecclerigg Crag. Just inshore of the cross, in a thick tangle of undergrowth, the curious visitor will discover some sloping rock faces bearing a series of mysterious inscriptions. A guide-book dating from the 1850's records some of the wording:

"A SLAVE LANDING ON THE BRITISH STRAND, BECOMES FREE." "THE LIBERTY OF THE PRESS." "1836. WILLIAM IV. PRESIDENT JACKSON. LOUIS PHILIPPE. BRITANNIA RULES THE WAVES." "NATIONAL DEBT £800,000,000. O SAVE MY COUNTRY, HEAVEN! GEORGE III. AND WILLIAM PITT." "MONEY IS THE SINEW OF WAR." "FIELD MARSHAL WELLINGTON. HEROIC ADMIRAL NELSON. CAPTAIN COOK. ADMIRAL RODNEY." "STEAM". One rock bears the legend: "1837 WORDSWORTH JOHN BOLTON Storrs Hall BOWNESS SCHOOL SHAW of the Life Guards at WATERLOO & C. JAMES BRANCKER George Warden GILES REDMAYN."

The letters, in some cases six inches tall, are cut deep into the rock with a perfection which few masons could hope to achieve. The enormity of the task is shown by the fact that some of the inscriptions have been embossed - ie. the rock has been chipped away from around the letters. Some writing is in Gothic script, but most is incised in ordinary Roman capitals.

The inscriptions date from the 1830's and are reputed to be the work of John Longmire of Troutbeck, described as a harmless eccentric. He spent some six years on his self-imposed task, working at it in all weathers, night and day. For well over a century the inscriptions lay completely forgotten, and indeed few people are aware of their existence even today. Lying in the private grounds of Ecclerigg House, they soon became covered by moss, earth, leaves, and it is only in recent times that the rocks have been cleaned off and restored.

It is sad to note that only a few years after Longmire had completed his work, some of these inscribed rocks were broken up, for this is where the stone for Wray Castle, just across the lake on the western shore, was quarried.

BELLE ISLE

> *Windermere is not all tales of doom and horror. Here is the true story of a genuine romance: how a young and beautiful heiress fell in love with and married the playmate of her childhood years, and of how they both lived happily ever afterwards - the story of Isabella Curwen of Belle Isle.*

The house of Curwen is an ancient one. It claims descent from one Ivo Tailbois, the reputed founder of Kendal Castle who was granted land in the area by William Rufus, while the name Curwen derives from Culwen in Galloway, where the family once owned large estates. The Curwens, however, were always associated historically with the town of Workington, where they had held the manor of Seaton since the 11th century and played a leading part in the affairs of West Cumberland. When Mary Queen of Scots crossed the Solway to England in 1568 she spent her first night at Workington Hall as the guest of the Curwens.

By 1778, however, the male line had come to an end and the only surviving member of the family was a fifteen-year-old girl, Isabella, a handsome young lady and heiress to a fortune of almost £34,000. She had had an unhappy childhood, having lost her mother just two years previously, and she hated London, where she was at school. Her beauty and her wealth, even at that relatively young age, made her one of the most sought-after heiresses in the county, but her heart was already lost to her childhood friend (and first cousin on her mother's side), John Christian.

The Christians were another well-to-do and influential family, living at Ewanrigg near Maryport. They had originally come over from the Isle of Man shortly after the Restoration, and quickly rose in the social sphere. Fletcher Christian, of mutiny on the Bounty fame, was John's first cousin on his father's side. John was an independent-minded young man, intelligent, ambitious, generous of spirit, and when he fell head-over-heels in love with his cousin Isabella, and she with him, it seemed nothing could stand in the way of their happiness. But as usual, there was a fly in the ointment: the fact that Isabella had been made a ward of court on the death of her father. Being still under 21 she needed the Lord Chancellor's permission to marry.

Although there was every indication that such permission would not be withheld, neither could endure the tedious wait which inevitably accompanies legal proceedings: love is never patient. John had returned from his travels in France and Switzerland in 1782, unable to remain away from his beloved for a moment longer. Desperately in love, they did what any spirited young couple would do in such circumstances: they ran away to Scotland. But no brief ceremony at the blacksmith's shop in Gretna Green for them: these were a couple with means, and a social position to uphold. They continued all the way to Edinburgh and were married there in the spring of that year, when Isabella was 19 and already a radiantly beautiful young woman. The couple's happiness was now complete. Matters were squared with the Lord Chancellor's office, and for the honeymoon they were able to repair to Isabella's (and now, of course, John's) new holiday home in the Lakes, which had been acquired on her behalf barely a year before. This was the island of Long Holme on Windermere.

Long Holme had undergone several changes of ownership through the 18th century. As we have seen, it passed from the Philipsons in 1739, and by 1774 it had ended up in the hands of a gentleman from Nottingham, Mr Thomas English. English was a successful businessman who decided that the most appropriate way to spend his wealth would be to move to the Lakes, purchase an island, build a house there and live in it. This, however, was to be no ordinary house; it was to be a rotunda, a round [or strictly speaking, cylindrical] house built after a style which had become very fashionable in Italy.

Thomas English was probably Windermere's first 'off-comer' - that is, a resident from outside the area - and was certainly the first gentleman to settle anywhere in the Lake District purely because he enjoyed the scenery. At that time the former Philipson residence, Holme House, was still in existence, but this was now demolished to make way for English's new mansion. It was while the foundations for this building were being excavated that pieces of armour and cannon balls were discovered, dating almost certainly from the period of the Civil War, when the Philipsons' house was under siege. Also unearthed were some pieces of mosaic flooring, thought to be the remains of a Roman villa which had stood on the island during the Roman occupation of Galava, the fort at Waterhead.

Mr English engaged the services of John Plaw, a famous London architect, and work began on the project right away, so that by 1778 the building was practically complete. It is the earliest house of such design in England - the more substantial Ickworth House in Suffolk was not begun until 1791. The round house is built of local stone, is three storeys high and capped by a dome, and has a diameter of 54 feet. On its eastern aspect there is a portico in classical style overlooking the lake, while carved figures representing the spirits of summer and autumn were found on either side of the door. At the apex of the dome is a lantern window which lights a spiral stairway in the centre of the building.

A house of Italian design, however, was not English's sole concern; he had plans for the entire island. All of Long Holme was to be reduced from its natural state into a country park. The island was practically bare of trees at this time; felling had been carried on since the early Middle Ages and large tracts of the island had been given over to cultivation. The soil is fertile, the land even, with no big outcrops of rock such as are found everywhere else in the district; a small area in the centre used to be a peat moss. 18th-century prints show the virtually treeless aspect of the island quite clearly, the only object of any distinction upon it being the house itself. In fact, only a few large oaks still remained of the dense woods which had originally covered Long Holme.

English planned a formal garden which was laid out to the north of the house, where the remains of the mosaic pavement were found. A fruit orchard with its enclosing wall was established; the whole island was planted with trees to reduce its bareness and at the same time make it appear larger than it actually was. To complete his work, a path of white sand around the periphery ran for a distance of over two miles. In all English spent over £6,000 in building and other improvements, a vast sum of money for those days, and as the writer Gilpin drily commented,

"...he has contrived to do almost every thing, that one would wish had been left undone".
Hutchinson wrote: *"The great island is little better than a bank of sand, and is now under the dispelling hand of a deformer".*

For Thomas English, in his enthusiasm to tame the hand of Nature, had violated practically every canon of the Picturesque, the aesthetic movement which was then fashionable amongst the cultivated classes. William Gilpin, the proponent of the movement, was the first to criticise the formal planning; he was closely followed by Hutchinson, who savagely attacked the lack of taste of both English and his architect, describing the house as:

"....A Dutch Burgomaster's palace", which, with its cabbage garden, *"...is so offensive to the traveller's eye, that he turns away in disgust".* Even the peripheral footpath gave offence for resembling *"...the dusty paths of foot passengers over Stepney Fields, or the way along which the owner has often heyed to Hackney".*

The famous guide book writer, Thomas West, was another who deplored the new developments on Long Holme, where:

"....the sweet secreted cottage is no more, and the sycamore grove is fled... an unpleasing contrast to the natural simplicity and insular beauty of the place".

It was a view which persisted for many years. H.S. Cowper, writing his history of Hawkshead over a hundred years later, took the opportunity while condemning Wray Castle to castigate English:
"It can but be that same mistaken eccentricity which induced Mr English to erect that strange enormity in architecture which

decorates Long Holme, or, as it is now called in exactly the same fantastic spirit, 'Belle Isle'."

Needless to say, the arch-conservationist William Wordsworth had a poor opinion of the house, and indeed of all such developments in general, writing in his Guide to the Lakes (1810):

"....the Islands of Derwent-water and Winandermere, as they offered the strongest temptation, were the first places seized upon, and were instantly defaced by the intrusion".

It is true that when the round house was first erected it could be seen for miles around, a kind of watch-tower or lighthouse dominating the approaches to Bowness Bay, standing sentinel over the central part of the lake. Denuded of trees the island was long, flat and uninteresting, and its novel form of architecture must have stuck out like a sore thumb. It must be remembered that apart from buildings of substance like Calgarth Hall or Rayrigg, this was the only large residence in an area whose usual habitation was a tiny cottage well hidden in the landscape, so that in a way it is not to be wondered at that 18th-century writers found the round house so offensive to the eye.

And yet, they were condemning a unique and beautiful building. Today Belle Isle's round house is one of the most attractive and interesting buildings in Windermere. Its shape and proportions are pleasing to the eye, it does not intrude but rather complements the landscape, and it is aesthetically satisfying: which is far more than can be said for many of the buildings which have sprung up to disfigure Bowness in recent years. For if those writers of old - Gilpin, Hutchinson, West, Wordsworth and so many more, could sail into Bowness Bay today and then walk up the road towards Windermere, they would surely be struck speechless with amazement and disbelief at what has been inflicted on this once lovely village in the name of commercial development.

English, however, did not stand completely alone. James Clarke, writing shortly afterwards, tore into the case for the picturesque with a devastating logic, commenting:

"Was he to take boat and sail for a walk in his garden when he had ten minutes to spare? Was he, when he wanted to read a few pages in his garden, to travel two miles to do it? Was his cook to fetch every handful of parsley, or other thing of that kind, cross the Lake, perhaps in a high wind? I have with pleasure fed upon delicious fruit pulled upon that island, the very spot where two years before grew nothing but briers and thorns".

J. Houseman also approved, writing in 1800:

"Sweet groves, pleasant walks, and verdant lawns, with a neat house, in a proper situation, and without one formal or direct line to offend the eye; all contribute towards its beauties".

The much-needed support, however, came too late. Poor Mr English, disheartened by the fierce criticism, faced in addition with business troubles and threatened with bankruptcy, gave up in despair. In 1781 he sold out - house, garden, island - and left the district, never to be heard of in Windermere again. The new owner was (as the reader may have guessed) Miss Isabella Curwen of Workington Hall. She had acquired a bargain: Long Holme sold for the sum of 1,640 guineas (or £1722), a remarkably low figure, even in those days, for so desirable a property.

Belle Isle Rotunda, c. 1984

Belle Isle

John Christian was able and ambitious, and on his marriage to the wealthy heiress of the Curwen estates his future was assured. He now had wealth and influence allied to his own native ability, and decided to give up the law (in which he had been trained) to enter politics, being elected Liberal M.P. for Carlisle in 1786. Later he became the member for Cumberland, which he succeeded in holding against strong opposition from the Conservative Lowthers. In 1790 he adopted his wife's surname and took the family arms, being henceforth known as John Christian Curwen.

As soon as Curwen was established on Long Holme he commenced a programme of improvements. The round house had not actually been completed when English left the island, but the new owners soon added the final touches. The formal garden was done away with, while tree-planting was undertaken on a large scale, including larch, Weymouth pine, ash and other species, all of which contribute to the fine stand of timber which today characterises Belle Isle - so much that in summer the round house is practically blocked out from the lake by foliage. A small stone rampart was built around the entire length of the shore to prevent wave erosion; sheep were introduced from the fells to keep the grass down. In fact by 1802 the property had improved so much that Curwen received an offer of £20,000 for it, more than ten times the price which had originally been paid.

He was not, however, without his critics; as Wordsworth was to criticise English, his sister Dorothy was equally outraged by Curwen's improvements. After a visit to Long Holme in 1802 she recorded in her Journal:

"It seems to me to be, however, no better than it was. They have made no natural glades; it is merely a lawn with a few miserable young trees, standing as if they were half-starved. There are no sheep, no cattle upon these lawns. It is neither one thing or another - neither natural, nor wholly cultivated and artificial, which it was before. And that great house! Mercy upon us! If it could be concealed, it would be well for all who are not pained to see the pleasantest of earthly spots deformed by man. But it cannot be covered. Even the tallest of our old oak trees would not reach to the top of it".

Although Curwen is remembered chiefly for his achievements in agriculture, particularly in West Cumberland, he was also a keen forester and it is in this context that he is important in the Windermere area. In the 1790s he had acquired a large tract of land along Claife Heights, including Heald and Crier Woods, generally known as 'Furness Fells'. It was on the whole waste land, unsuited for agriculture because of its steep fall towards the lake and numerous rocky outcrops - the reader may recall it was here that the ghostly Claife Crier was ultimately laid. Later growth of woodland has totally screened the face of this hillside, but early writers who used the word "precipitous" to describe it were not always exaggerating, for in many places the slope falls steeply and abruptly from the crags which outcrop along the length of Claife. Indeed, the very name comes from the Norse *kleif*, a cliff.

Furness Fells had always had a sprinkling of trees, mainly the native English varieties such as yew, holly, birch, hazel. Curwen now proceeded to create a full English woodland, planting the hillside between the ferry and Belle Grange with tens of thousands of saplings including practically the whole range of deciduous trees then growing in Britain, a fact reflected in the variety of this splendid woodland which has today reached full maturity. The species on which he concentrated, however, was larch. In the 18th century this tree had only just been introduced into the Lake District from the continent and quickly became popular with landowners, who saw it as a source of profit as well as having some aesthetic value.

The reason for the sudden popularity of larch is not difficult to find. England's vast woodland cover of native oak was in steep decline and planting could not keep pace. The heavy demand for oak for use in ship-building during the Napoleonic Wars made the situation even worse, and it was thought at the time that the quick-growing larch might prove a useful substitute, and its cultivation was encouraged. Curwen in fact managed to persuade Parliament to offer an award to the man who planted the most larch trees, and then went on to win it himself!

The strength and durability of oak, however, could only be matched by steel, which was eventually to replace it in ship-building. The use of larch for boats was confined to an area nearer home - the Lake District itself. The locally-built boats which in later years plied for hire on the major lakes such as Windermere and Derwentwater all came to be built of larch, from small rowing boats to large passenger-carrying launches. Indeed, larch is still the material out of which rowing boats are constructed, although in commercial launches it has been replaced by tropical hardwoods such as teak or iroka.

Curwen in due course completed his possessions by acquiring the Great Boat estate (ie. the Windermere ferry and the Ferry Inn) and Station Scar, the hillside above. He also constructed a new road through the woods between Belle Grange and the village of High Wray; the old one can still be followed as a track along the lake shore past Red Nab and Pinstones - nowadays a popular route for mountain bikers. Belle Grange had in fact been included with the original purchase of Long Holme by Thomas English, who completed the residence in 1778, intending it for use as a dower-house.

So much is heard of John Curwen in connection with Windermere that it might be taken for granted that Long Holme was his usual residence. Yet when not attending to his parliamentary duties at Westminster, both he and Isabella lived at her ancestral home - Workington Hall. The round house at Windermere was for the summer months only - a holiday home in the Lakes. It remained, however, their favourite spot. In 1813, on a visit to the lakes of Killarney, John wrote to Isabella:

"I could not hide from my own heart, not will I disguise it from you, how much I apprehended lest I should now be compelled to acknowledge there was a spot on the surface of this habitable globe more enchanting than Windermere".

So fond indeed was he of Windermere that he renamed the island. Instead of Long Holme, by which it had been known since medieval times, he started referring to it as 'Bella' Isle, after his beloved Isabella. For a while he was alone in this usage, for throughout the 19th century, guide-book writers without exception would refer to it as 'Curwen Island', or even sometimes as 'Christian Island'. His own pet name, however, was the one which eventually prevailed. Belle Isle was first recorded on a map in 1823 and soon established itself in popular usage, certainly assisted by confusion with the French *belle* for 'beautiful', and so replacing the traditional Long Holme.

Belle Isle, or Curwen Island, quickly became a popular tourist attraction. It had always been a focus of attention on Windermere; but now the completion of the round house and the additional attraction of Curwen's landscape improvements meant that Long Holme became a definite 'must' for everyone visiting the Lakes. In 1792, for instance, Adam Walker wrote of his visit to Long Holme:

"CALYPSO and her Nymphs surprized the ship-wrecked TELEMACHUS [sic] with threats, but we were more fortunate on this Island; for a beautiful group, including the LADY of the ISLAND and her sweet CHIDDREN, came with much politeness, and pressed us to partake of their dessert.... and much we lamented that our time would not permit a compliance with their wishes to detain us a few days".

Joseph Budworth, visiting at around the same time, wrote:

"About one we landed upon Thompson's Island, from which we have fair sight of Belle-isle House and pleasure grounds, appearing to be laid out in much modern taste; this island is near two others, called Lilies of the Valley, which are deserving of their name, for they are beautiful little spots".

Throughout the 19th century tourists flocked to the island in ever increasing numbers; some of the Bowness hotels sold tickets which visitors could use to gain admission, but by 1884 the house and island had been let privately, and unauthorised landing was discouraged. This was understandable in view of the increasing frequency of tourists visiting Windermere. In earlier times they were few in number and usually on the same social scale as the Curwens, since only the wealthier classes had the leisure or the means to travel. As time went on, however, the number of visitors rose as their class fell, and when in the 1890s Bowness began to be flooded with working class families from the northern industrial cities during the summer holidays, it would of course have been quite out of the question to permit such persons on the island!

Included in the original purchase of Long Holme had been a number of smaller islands which nobody else seemed to want: these were Hawes Holme, Thompson Holme, the two Lilies of the Valley, Maiden Holme, Crow Holme, as well as two islets virtually linked with the main island - Snake Holme and Fir Holme. These all remained with the family until the big break-up of the Curwen estates in Windermere in 1964, when the properties on Claife went to the National Trust, while the islands (except Snake Holme and Fir Holme) were ceded to the Lake District Special Planning Board. The Great Boat property (Windermere ferry) remained with the family until 1948, when it was taken over by the joint Westmorland and Lancashire county councils; the ferry is now operated by Cumbria County Council.

For 210 years Belle Isle formed part of the Curwen family estates, inhabited by the descendants of John and Isabella, although for much of that period the house was in use only as a summer home. In the 1970s and '80s the island was opened up for visitors, including conducted tours of the round house, but later these were, sadly, discontinued; instead a conference centre was opened in 1988. In the early spring of 1991 Belle Isle passed from the Curwen family after a long and historic association, and was sold to Mr and Mrs Harold Lefton for a sum believed to be in the region of several million pounds - many, many times the 1,640 guineas which had originally been paid for it.

As a sad footnote to the story of Belle Isle occurred in 1994, two days before Christmas, when the entire dome and upper storey of the rotunda were destroyed by fire. How the Windermere fire service managed to transport their equipment across the lake, at night, and save the remainder of the building and its contents, is a legend in itself. The building was under wraps for almost three years before a completely new dome and upper works were revealed, resplendent in the autumn sunshine, a good - if not altogether true - likeness of the original.

CONCLUSION

In addition to stories such as the Claife Crier or the Calgarth Skulls, Windermere has other legends of the terrifying and the bizarre. Less well-known perhaps, but no less horrific, are the Basswicks boggle (a boggle being the local term for a hobgoblin or similar demonic manifestation) which allegedly haunted Graythwaite woods on the west shore of the lake to confront travellers returning after dark from the ferry. The Beech Hill boggle was its opposite number which would stalk belated travellers on the eastern shore. There were also tales of a phantom boat which sailed the lake on dark and misty nights to terrify the lone fisherman, crewed and navigated by ghouls, its approach heralded by shrieks and wailings, replete with scenes of diabolical horror.

Yet there are tales of less baneful beings. One such is the legendary Cornelius, described variously as a fugitive from justice, or a sailor from a ship in the Armada which was supposedly wrecked off Maryport. He made his dwelling at Blakeholme Wray (later known as Cornelius Bluff), the high crag south of Blake Holme at the foot of Gummers How. Here his *'Shoppe'* is still to be found: a small stone hut, twelve feet square and seven feet high with a small, low window and a hearth and chimney against the rock face. Only twenty yards from the lake shore, it is covered with ivy and hidden by undergrowth, quite invisible from the water. Until the 1930s Cornelius Shop was used regularly as a temporary shelter by wood-cutters who would visit these woods every fifteen years or so to coppice the young trees. The landowner, the late Sir John Fisher, always insisted that the shelter remain exactly as it was. Another story, however, makes out that Cornelius was a watch-repairer, preferring to carry out his trade in this remote and sheltered spot.

The story which has Cornelius as a fugitive from justice also gives him a hoard of treasure to hide away, the proceeds from his days of outlawry. This is, appropriately, buried on Silver Holme, the small island not far away on the western shore below

Conclusion

Graythwaite. Here, perhaps concealed on the lake bed nearby, there *'liggs a kist o'silver'*, waiting for some lucky person to dig it up and make his fortune. But Silver Holme has a more prosaic origin: it comes from a Norse personal name, Solva; *Solvar Holmr* means 'Solva's Island'.

Windermere has a long and eventful past, not just the black and white of historical records but also the colourful skein of mystery and romance weaving through the years to add its own background to ordinary events. Did the ferryman perhaps die of a simple heart attack? Were just a couple of mouldered skulls discovered at Calgarth? Was a wealthy businessman hounded in later life by memories of a violent and mis-spent youth? The prosaic is rejected for the supernatural: a diabolical manifestation sent the boatman to his grave, a dying curse spat from the lips of one desperate for revenge caused those skulls to manifest, or those severed hands to rise from the water.

It is hard to feel terror of the unknown in broad daylight when the sun shines down on Windermere and the lake is full of boats of every description, when the breeze rustles gently in the woodlands and the fells rise peacefully in the distance. But on a stormy night, when the face of the deep is enraged by the howling gale, when the rain beats relentlessly down, when the trees are bent by the storm, when winter bares its savage teeth, where is that sunlit calm and tranquillity?

On such a night the Crier is allowed to roam; small wonder that the road winding over Claife from Hawkshead to Belle Grange (with Calgarth Hall a scant mile away across the water) was shunned at night. Small wonder that travellers would listen to the gale roaring through the swaying branches and think they heard the voice of the Crier as, released from his ancient prison, he stood once more at the water's edge to strike terror and death into the soul of any who dared to cross the lake on that wild night!

BIBLIOGRAPHY

AITCHISON, G.	Calgarth Hall. CW2, 1935
BEARD, Geoffrey	The greater house in Cumbria. Westmorland Gazette, 1978
BOUCH, C.M.L.	Prelates and people of the lake counties. Titus Wilson, 1948
BRIGGS, J.	The Lonsdale Magazine, Vol. 2. 1821
BUDWORTH, J.	A fortnight's ramble to the Lakes.... 1792
CLARKE, James	A survey of the lakes. 1787
COLLINGWOOD, W.G.	"The Fatall Nuptiall"... By Richard Braithwaite. CW2, 1913
COLLINGWOOD, W.G.	The Lake Counties. Dent, 1932
COWPER, H.S.	Hawkshead. Bemrose, 1899
CURWEN, J.F.	A history of the ancient house of Curwen. Titus Wilson, 1928
EVANS, Arthur	Lake County Villains. Red Earth Publications, 1993
FAHY, T.G.	The Philipson family: Part I. Philipson of Calgarth. CW2, 1964
GIBSON, A. Craig	The Lakeland of Lancashire. THSLC, Vol. 6, 1865
GILPIN, William	Observations, relative chiefly to Picturesque Beauty, made in the year 1772...
HOUSMAN, J.	A descriptive tour and guide to the lakes.... Carlisle, 1800
HUGHES, E.	North country life in the 18th century. Vol. II. Oxford University Press, 1965
HUTCHINSON, W.	An excursion to the lakes in Westmorland and Cumberland.1776
JONES, Clement	John Bolton of Storrs. Titus Wilson, 1959
LONSDALE, H.	The worthies of Cumberland. 1867
MACKAY, C.	The scenery and poetry of the English Lakes. Longmans, 1852
MACHELL, Thomas	Antiquary on horseback. CWAAS, 1963
MARTINEAU, Harriet	A complete guide to the English lakes. 1955
MILLS, H.V.	Lake country romances. Stock, 1892
THOMPSON, B.L.	The Windermere ferry: an antiquarian essay. Titus Wilson, 1971
THOMPSON, T.W.	Wordsworth's Hawkshead. Oxford University Press, 1970
TULLIE, Isaac	A narrative of the siege of Carlisle in 1644 and 1645. 1840
WALKER, A.	Remarks made in a tour... To the lakes of Westmorland... 1792
WEST, Thomas	A guide to the lakes in Cumberland, Westmorland, and Lancashire. 4th ed. 1789
WHITE, J.P.	Lays and legends of the English Lake country. 1873
WORDSWORTH, Dorothy	The Grasmere Journals, 1800-1803
WORDSWORTH, William	A guide to the lakes. 1810

Notes

CW2: Transactions of the Cumberland and Westmorland Antiquarian and Archaeological Society, Series 2
THSLC: Transactions of the Historic Society of Lancashire and Cheshire. New Series
CWAAS: Transactions of the Cumberland and Westmorland Antiquarian and Archaeological Society, Occasional Series